Unsteady

Also by Monique Ferrell

Black Body Parts, Cross+Roads Press, 2010

w/Julian L. Williams, *Her Own Worst Enemy: The Eternal Internal Gender Wars of Our Sisters,* forthcoming 2012

w/Julian L. Williams, *Lead, Follow, Or Move Out of the Way: Global Perspectives in Literature,* Third Edition.

w/Julian L. Williams and Mark Noonan, *Good Writing Made Simple,* Second Edition.

Unsteady

Monique Ferrell

 Books

The New York Quarterly Foundation, Inc.
New York, New York

NYQ Books™ is an imprint of The New York Quarterly Foundation, Inc.

The New York Quarterly Foundation, Inc.
P. O. Box 2015
Old Chelsea Station
New York, NY 10113

www.nyqbooks.org

Copyright © 2011 by Monique Ferrell

All rights reserved. No part of this book may be used or reproduced in any manner whatsoever without written permission of the author.

First Edition

Set in New Baskerville

Layout and Design by Raymond P. Hammond
Cover Photo and Design by Patricia Jade Persaud | www.patriciapersaud.com
Author Photo ©2011 Julian Williams

Library of Congress Control Number: 2011942031

ISBN: 978-1-935520-53-5

Unsteady

Acknowledgments

epitafios—*Cimarron Review*
all there is—*Pinyon Review*
eek—*Pinyon Review*
how to write a woman—*Valley Voices Review*
tyler perry would love this—*North American Review*
unsteady—forthcoming *Lullwater Review*
they say this is a love poem too—*New York Quarterly*

For Mark, who once told me that I would never,
and for Ai and Lisa who always told me that I would.

Contents

idolatry

touch   /   *13*
epitafios   /   *15*
all there is…   /   *18*
eek   /   *21*
how to write a woman   /   *23*
to live with regret   /   *25*

crescendo

the boxer   /   *29*
the deadliest catch was you   /   *32*
lena   /   *34*
tyler perry would love this   /   *36*
tennessee   /   *40*
inaugural: what we've been trying to say since then   /   *42*
mean mugging   /   *45*

unnatural disasters

call back the waters   /   *49*
little girls…   /   *54*
chi-town   /   *57*
sak pasé   /   *61*
to see the world   /   *63*

unsteady

unsteady   /   *67*
brooklyn state of mind: the caterpillar poem   /   *70*
they say this is a love poem too…   /   *73*
cradle board   /   *76*
snapped   /   *78*

idolatry

touch

I believe   that every space on earth   has memory my therapist says
this is true of our muscles   and tells me regularly   it is why
she has chosen   this profession

hurrying   people into wellness teaching the physically abused to break
free from the ties that bound and broke the skin   wanting them   to release
the atrophied   lukewarm memory   or chilling feel   of a clenched fist
bashing   down on *stillformingbone*   or challenging a much too sad heart

into surrendering   its burden at one fifty an hour for fifty minutes   each
week *best to do it now* she says *before the clock runs out   and your pockets
have gone thread bare we are at the dawn of a recession   the world
is threatening to end in 2012   and a black man   is running for president*

*you   do not have time for sadness our impolite world   is either   coming apart
at the seams   or jump starting   towards something   marvelous   whatever it is
don't you   want to feel it   to truly bear witness   with the totality   of your
nerve endings   and a well healed   new truth about your self*

who the fuck talks like this   I am thinking today   and why am I here   paying her my good money
didn't she hear me say that I've got some shit   on my mind   and on my chest that does not
go away   will not stay gone   after I leave her   with one of my   well-written checks

is she mad   they are not   going to let that black man become president

I wish   I had a drinking problem   but I'm a light weight   a two drink drunk
who likes to crawl into bed   after telling everyone how much I love them

what a wasted youth   I could have been promiscuous   a *bad* bad girl giving boys
hand jobs and head   behind the bleachers maybe smoking weed would have been
a good calling   a deep intoxicating inhale   room filled with empty dime bags and
visine to *get the red out* sparing   the prying eyes of my southern grandmother

had I relinquished   the drought of my spirit this way   perhaps these taut mounds
beneath the skin   wouldn't feel   so bad

experiencing   what I call muscle tone dementia recalling so many
old bad things almost every other day

walking through macy's   still makes me   clench my teeth   *justforasecond*

and then I come back again   and think about   how *successful* my therapist keeps
telling me I am and I turn my mind   to the *important* things   I am there to buy
a dress   for a special occasion   housewares for my home where   no one turns off
the lights   makes me feel unsafe   and there is always   food on the table

and this multi-billion dollar conglomerate in which I own no stock is not
the place where my father abandoned me   when I was seven

this is good   my therapist would say   *you are reclaiming space and memory   have
released a layer of sad muscle   really* I'd say to her in that smart-assed tone I reserve
just for these moments   *I was thinking I need to keep my ass out of macy's*

but I do things her way instead   because really I do not wish to be cruel
and unseemly one day I am going to be old and grey and I do not want
trick-or-treating children to shy away from the door

I don't want my *somedaychildren* writing letters to oprah about me about the
condition of their childhood   so I do things her way carrying my department
store packages into the subway with yet another reclaimed memory

and slide between two people who are willing to make room for me and my
inner child and I notice that we are all   closer than we need to be

knees touching elbows and un-cautioned thoughts overlapping and we   are stealing
a moment to feel something that isn't   damaged or broken   bits of a silly side
conversation   a glance at someone's newspaper   a slipping note from our neighbor's
earphones   it is all touch   and longing on this ride headed downtown

each one of us   making it   the best we know how

epitafios

billie holiday, dorothy dandrige, and josephine baker

I.
out of all the ways   I could have told you I was beautiful
I had to sing it to you   deep and slow
voice tinted   with a hazy melancholy   all the grief and grandeur
I'd ever known   thrown in for good measure

what a sight I must have been to you   an *I didn't know colored girls could do that*
kind of thing   all beat up and tragic   just to make things interesting

I can tell you   a thing or two   about stilling   the ebb of the encroaching madness
how to pour it easy   into a glass over the ice alongside the whisky   while
what is left of your dreams   burns the back of your throat

this is how you silence   the unforgiveable memory   of bad luck and too wrong
decisions that haunt the insides of your mind's eye   in the morning noon   and night
and the *almosteverytime* they insist upon rearing   their lovely bloody memories

I know death to be finite   but memory is a dangerous dark-hearted corpse   that
will not stay buried   shaming you into awakeness when the world is still sleepy
and you are straining hard against the thick silence   listening with your whole body
eager to find somebody *any* body another pulse an inhale exhale besides your own

oh the mind is a crowded   decadent thing   that will not grant you any reprieve

and so   I never knew how to be anything   but what I was   the best and worst
of my circumstances   laid thread bare   against a soundtrack   my pain   made easy
in melody   and didn't you like it   the *sicksadness* of it all

head low   bowed over the lyrics   all about the man who did me wrong
the love   I could never lay claim to

too many wrong hands   each touching   in the *don't you dare touch there* places
a belly filled instead   with old negro spirituals in the place where   three square meals
should have been   a little slap and tickle   for a payment and price   or even a promise

life for me had never been no crystal staircase but was instead a chasm   wide with
I don't knows and regret   and   every now and again

some music   to move the blues along

II.
It had to come to this   this deep laid low feeling as the tide runs out on your life
ushered   into this world   all unhurried   head full   of promise and expectation
and here I had to leave it   as a laugh-line on someone else's face
a tick in the collective memory   all too quickly   and by accident

should have burned much brighter   than I did   girls like me   dipped in
black velvet   should get more   out of life   ought to be able to cash in
on sunsets and all things offered   that do not include scraps
from   somebody else's plate

should have been able to play cards with the devil   at his very own table   and
live to tell the story   on a tomorrow   over some fancy colored drink   with exotic fruit
and umbrellas   that dizzy up your world   while the inside sweetness   oozes over the
sides   onto your hands   that are so full of promise and expectation

not this laid low   in my own filth   body exposed to the world

and *that* is what I was thinking   in the moment   hands outstretched like jesus
on the cross   on the floor   feeling vulnerable   and shabby   inside my black velvet
once a star   a catch in someone's breath   a double take   the aching want
between a man's thighs   wasn't   I something

pushing   past the crimes against me   thrown up against a wall   like an elegant spitball
been used up   and left for dead   in the deep down places   wasn't expected to be
nothing but a never was   and yet   I was   somebody   a colossus   badass grand dame

a sacred silhouette of my own making

and god had nothing to do with it   it was pure spite   and desperation   that made
me climb up on out   of the sewer   of low expectation   up out into a world
that was not built for me

and there should have been more   for all us children   dipped in black velvet
little girls like me   who became women   because what else   was there for us to do

and   on the occasion   of our living and dying   somehow the skies   should have   burned
a little less brightly   the planet should have spun   with a little less certainty   some
homage paid   for those of us   who wished to be bigger   than our own bodies

III.
bronze venus black pearl   créole goddess   la baker
such a head trip for the funny faced girl with the banana skirt

born under the right sign   I was

everyone   needs two faces one to greet the world   the other to survive it

one to play pretend   in the alley ways   that your hands are not leafing through
your neighbor's garbage   the unwanted refuse of their lives   as you smile your way
through the stench   biting down hard   on whatever will still
the emboldened thunder   in your

swollen gut   one to wear   a water color smile   as you step out of the cardboard
box   that is your home   uneasy sleep   still matted in the corners of your eyes
right on out into   the hard blue world   that is all but absent of you

my momma's cries about a colored girl's life being *a road of can't do to won't never*
on   either side of me

hell   I was born to be impossible to be this big   on paper   even better
live and in person   a phantasm   white hot to the touch   imagine that

and you could never know   what a fantastic leap of the imagination it took for me
to get here   learning to love a body   that was   all the time dual in nature
wanted and craved by you in the night   but in truth of day
a granddaughter   of struck down muted mule slaves   at your *beck and call*

all the time singing you   a song   throaty and melancholy a brown goddess
with a *praise jesus*   rise and fall in her breasts   while all the time   backstaging
it through kitchens and trap doors   'cause the front ones wouldn't have me

all the time   all the time   for you   being this thing   to keep you coming
wanting   needing   your *hourglassbaby* strutting   shaking   shimmying

sliding across any floor   any stage

looking for home   in your arms   the gaps in between   your teeth full of praise

it takes two faces to survive   with me   in my world   one to know the truth of things
and the other   to love me   in spite of them

all there is...

so powerful   is the emotion
that an author put pen to paper
telling the tale of two fig trees
growing   side by side   in rural america
so thick with love   no other choice
but to grow   into one another's arms

later   that same day   because there was more to say on the subject
of love   and the unfathomable
it occurred to her
to write the tale   of a rock formation   in the desert
shaded into the figure   of a man and woman
the two   so intertwined   that one
can never be distinguished from the other

and they are   always loving

it is that way   love
will either build you up or decimate you

the soul can only bear either of the two extremes

and I guess   I know what that means   I could be that fig tree   growing
into his arms
an insatiable   jealous lover
always reaching   concerned only with   my lover's boughs
never shading
any   other

and I could learn to love   hot upon the desert sand
carved to be my lover's likeness   thirsting   only after his body
loving   hard   against   the *desertcolored* sky
and every lost soul would marvel
at just   the thought of us

fall   transfixed   unable to lead themselves away
held fast by the sight

love is reckless that way

like food to an undernourished belly

is what we are never free from
what we never get enough of

even in a room filled with people
or a bed heavy with the weight of another

we are never loved enough
bold enough to ask that we be loved properly

so we spend a lifetime
making others suffer   for what is deficient in us

and then   they don't get enough love either

love is redundant that way

but how do you ask to be loved
to be seen

shouldn't it be expected   a given

I guess   the best that we can do
is imagine love
passing on what feel like   impossible stories
about fig trees   and desert wonders   or

like this one…

in oklahoma
an indian man rose from his bed
on valentine's day

no money for a gift   for his sweetheart
just enough government commodities   to last the month

with nothing to buy his wife of fifty-five years
he literally gave her   his last breath
died
mowing her name into the grass of their lawn

(and this was a good death   young warriors leave the tribe for a good
death such as this one   a meaningful life   death in pursuit of something
more profound)

and his beloved   upon seeing him through the picture window

phone in her hand
screamed   letting the receiver fall to the floor
drawing out their neighbors

she   called his name   one final time

and had the sense enough to follow her lover's soul

because who could or would   ever love her
that perfectly   again

now tell me

who wouldn't   do the same

eek

I understand now   what it is I feel for you
poised over your broken fleeing body with a skillet

even I have the capacity for death

more than three thousand times your size   you unnerve me
because you will not bend to my will

in louisiana   after the flood waters receded
and the ninth ward did its best to recover
the bravest of its citizens   rose from the soot and mildew

but you and your kind   did them all one better
doubling   tripling   in size and mass so much so
that the national guard has a unit dedicated to your erasure

forget the gang violence   new orleans as a murder capital
the sheer decimation

it is you we cannot abide

they tell us   that should the world implode
as worlds are apt to do
you and the roaches will survive us all
make yourselves immune to famine and plague   even to us

and   this is why we cannot *abide* you
you defy logic   the rules of engagement for master and slave
superior and inferior
two-legged over four-legged   and feathered

you will not behave
force us to face our certain mortality

we hold your lives in the balance using human understanding
to build the better mouse trap

and even then at best   our resistance to your superiority is futile

for you want us to know what death is
not throw the brick and hide our hands

you die defiantly messy   rude   flavored with hostility a willingness to gnaw off your own appendages

have your spines broken in two   decompose inside our walls
behind the lovely wallpaper

this   you seem to say   is the price of death   the rewards of so-called humanity
the perks of being human
you cannot send me abroad with a gun in my hand
only to return with a lovely flag-draped coffin

but   as we strive to rid the planet of you   we deny   that we are
the greatest pestilence   earth has ever known

and I know this to be true   watching you writhe and twitch
eyes still searching for an escape
skin burning with the poison I set out for you

as if you were a beloved pet

I wonder for a moment what that same poison
has contributed to the air the water my lungs
in what way the ramifications   of *this* action   will revisit my door
some   future day
but I cannot help myself   we cannot co-exist together
humanity   despite its beauty   is destined to destroy itself and others
destroy itself   because it destroys others

so I like   my ancestors before me   kill   that I may live

how to write a woman

an ode to tennessee williams

if you were any other man   with harsh and ridiculous stroke of key   or pen
you would have painted them   this way

to be a man's likeness   his compliment
non judgmental   or   perhaps   very much so
as the hero's silly ally   or as the venom in his bones

the gal pal   ever longing on the sidelines of his life
his equal on a football field   a master at the crack of the bat
perhaps a lover   unequaled to any   before her   or after
an all consuming great orgasm who   every now and again
through the embers of memory   still play his spine   like piano keys

divine   an illusion   the one who got away

but   because you were *him*
and for you restraint was a suggestion   sin a delightful invitation

a woman's life was but a battle cry
Eve folded in on herself   and because she is Eve
a little miffed at the grave injustice visited upon her sisters
you allowed yourself to become our beautiful muse

and because you were *him*

filled them instead with spite   and animus

big hair first names that sound like accusations

said behind   hand fans   covering signifying smiles   on a veranda
in the summer heat
mint and honeysuckle   fermenting the air
short *tightsoundingnames* that *claw catch* the leaves
and whisper their devilment

blanche   maggie   stellaaa…

fashioned to be   the mirror into a man's soul   into his darkest heart
the booze   sadism   loss and lust   even his enchanted sadness

and each one   with the turn of her head   arched back   or the closing off or lashing out

into her own madness
gave the women watching or reading   one simple option

to not make men more complicated than they are
no more a hero or magnanimous   than woman herself

but   merely a man

and because you made them *overthetop*
you stripped away the victim status

laid them evenly on the battle field   breast bone to breast bone
insisting that the heaviness of their lives be seen and witnessed

knowing fully   and all too well
that a woman   a real woman   unknown to herself   and dismissive of her demons

can never survive in the light

off of the page
into any reality
or be safe   inside her own footsteps

to live with regret

if you spend enough time   in the company of women
eventually   they will lay down their souls

and what they confess is sometimes unexpected   thrown in amid
their reflections   on bad dates   god awful sex   and remember whens

and just when   everything feels easy   and you are grateful
for your girlfriends   happy that there is someone   *aroomfull*
of someones   with which you can commiserate

one of them   lays herself low

I've been told   we are only as sick as our secrets   and that there is safety
in numbers   so   then and there   it seems right to speak a truth

and we know how to crawl down   onto the carpets or the tiled floors
in a house or an apartment   past the empty bottles   cups of ice
and pizza boxes   forming   once again   the amen choir   granting the
the confessor penance and peace   a temporary reprieve   from the ancient hurt

face down   limbs spread like a drunken false christ without a cross
a guttural moaning   of what sounds like mercy   is really the word   murder

an admittance that she placed the lit cigarette between those cracked lips
body   wasting away   from AIDS and drug addiction

her sister's   jet black locks splayed about her head   and the *hospitalwhite* pillow
what a beauty she used to be   all of the boys   whistling
as she walked that affected walk   developed   to make even the heads
of little old ladies   seated at their windows   *tisktisk*   at the sight of it

but there was also the blame and beatings   she took on her sister's behalf
because mommy would not believe   her beloved
firstborn daughter   guilty of any offense

no comfort for the good *still living*   second daughter   a virgin   until she married
in church every sunday   a good   catholic girl   just what felt like a deep one sided
maternal wishing   for the daughters   to exchange places

and who could stand to be so muted   in a room filled with chatter and fawning

so   she gave her that cigarette   because she asked for it   because she was always

sneaking them anyway   but   also   because she wanted   to shut   her mouth
felt a little smug   almost self-satisfied for a fraction of a second   that the mighty
had been brought so low   but   she crossed herself   like a good catholic girl
wishing away   the basic human instinct to survive   or be cherished

and instead   walked away   leaving her alone in the house   forgetting that oxygen
flames   and sleep   are enemies   as are often   mothers daughters   sisters
and   memory

and it didn't matter that the doctors gave her sister   merely weeks more to live
or that the authorities found no malice in the action   when you are a good daughter

what matters   is what you *think* you owe

whether or not you can enter   the gates of heaven unblemished   worried
that your mother will get there first   and bear false witness

and that   even in heaven

they will still   have each other   and like the good daughter

you will stand off   to the side

and   there before the face of god   still expect   nothing

Crescendo

the boxer

I.
Alpha

did somebody tell you   you had the world in your hands
that a mighty fist   is the only way to carve out a place   for yourself

when your blackness is unforgivable

but when your blackness *is* unforgivable
it is most difficult   to move out of your own way

despite the inclination to do otherwise

you know you are your own worst enemy

but what a ride into the great abyss it would be
dragging the entire world to hell with you

burn this black skin   you must have thought
and the house that built it along with it

and how could the forefathers have ever known   that all the anger
there would ever be in the world   would be fashioned   in the hull of a slave ship

crystallized into a living *burning white flame* under jim crow
and given legitimacy   to express itself   through the might of a boxing glove

didn't they know   you wanted blood   wanted your very own two fists   to pile drive
all white men   into their graves   wanted them humiliated   and so
you fucked their women   called them your wives   when it was illegal to do so

Jack Johnson   heavy weight champion of the world   inside a white man's design

how   did it still the voices in your head   as you lay beside her

her porcelain arm about your chest   limbs indistinguishable from your own
thick arm   used earlier in the day   to conduct your dark art

now   *lyinglazy* between her thighs

did you imagine that they would allow you to rest
that you could emerge from this novel unscathed

that there was yet more magic in your gloves beyond brutality

that you could create an alternate universe
one without devastation   an *I told you* so ending

but this was not meant to be   there was only one way to end the plotline

exiled   humiliated   disgraced   the embers of your life wrapped around
the tree trunk and broken bits of car that called you to some otherness

a cautionary tale of the world that was not built for you

your existence   tinted and framed with limitations   and loopholes
a can't do   to won't never   bargain with the devil

II.
EXODUS
(Mike Tyson)

and just what are you   now   sitting on a sound stage
across from oprah winfrey broken   sans money   a title

a man   unable to cry without the full magnitude of his body giving way

it makes you uncomfortable to cry   it made us *all* uncomfortable   watching you
bowed   as the flashback of your life played uncensored
against the folds of your mind's eye   *who is this man*   you said   *I don't trust him either*

are we to paint you with gentle lines   now   offer you our forgiveness
the hubris of man demands your flesh   and what's left of your future

we wish to inherit it all   we want your head   your body splayed before us

but it's so difficult to *want* anything from you now   what you have left to give
you owe to your maker   but   the boy in you   that we discarded   so very long ago
has issued us a bill   and it is   past due

this is what happens when a child is left alone forget the village

it takes the sheer force of the universe   to keep a child's eyes   open wide

I guess it was the bullies of your world   who first taught you to fight
having beat you each day   simply   because

I wonder   what each night
must have been for you   awaiting a fresh hell   watching the hours
unravel into yet another Bed-Stuy morning   only semi closed   your mind's eye focused
on your beloved pigeons kept safe   from the piss and stench side of brooklyn
that so many live   but too few   really talk about

and what was it   that killed   the little boy in you   the tiny piece of magic
you managed to keep safe   when no child should be asked to manage such a task

was it the sight of blood   the broken body of a beloved thing

that   like you   could not fight back

until *that* moment   unable to be *you* anymore   they took
the only thing   that has ever kept a man human   that which he loves

and this   is what closed your eyes completely   ground them down into fine slits
leaving only enough room to watch for the approach of the enemy

and we validated   if not your pain   the brutality with which you
expelled it   from your   life

and paid you handsomely for your efforts

don't cry mike   be a warrior   the trainers said
and then   fashioned your body   into a battering ram

but they should have made you   name your fists
maybe the left one grace   the other mercy

perhaps doing so   would have reminded you
that you deserved a little of each for yourself

and so did the people you came into contact with

before the drugs   jail
your questionable behavior with the women in your life

before you learned   that you cannot always live   on top of the world
didn't deserve to be confined to the bottom of the ocean

but deserved   a sliver of peace   somewhere in the middle

the deadliest catch was you

Captain Phillip Harris the Cornelia Marie and the Bering Sea

you knew what a real love affair was   didn't you   men are sometimes sick
with lust quite often   with the wrong one   and for many   a wrong reason

it must be something   to be so certain   knowing who   and   what you love
and how you'd give your life over to the nearly midnight waters changing
season   after season   just for   love's best caress

we laugh about men and their machines but maybe they know something
we women don't   there is a certainty as they stroke   the gears rods and
pistons   and what do we know   every turn of the engine   could most certainly
be an   unfailing   uncompromised   sigh of *neverending* requited   love

I never thought I'd see a man love two entities   that seemed to enjoy   even
relish   in the complicated   and dangerous threesome   I am no fool

the water is a strange goddess who is not to be toyed with   I curtsey before her
bowing low   respectful of her love   power and judgment   but you liked your

women   powerful raw untethered   just on the brink of letting it all go
while blindfolded   how you must have met   many a bering sea night

your crew asleep below   strangely   and especially fatigued   with what could only be
attributed   to her magic all of them   now   lulled   into twilight   by the fullness of her

while a silhouette wave   bodied like a woman   danced across the deck   before you
for your deep pleasure   then   moody and sure of herself
your other grand baby confident beneath   your bare feet   exhaled out a pointed
and sharp love song about sharing her man across time and water   and liking it

cigarette smoke   filling the captain's lair   your calloused hands   across the wheel
touch her tenderly   and the blessed   *crystalcold* water below   cleanses her   and
you   move this way   together

who   are we kidding   *this* is making love   and it is everything to you   a sweet
silent orgasm free of regrets and   *I'vechangedmyminds*   and then when everyone
is full and satiated   and the first light begins to signal its arrival   the voices of

a still *sleepdrunk* crew   waft up through the floorboards telling of *beyondbelief* dreams
about magnificent women   made of water and fire at the same time   who made
them laugh   and held them close while they cried   and unburdened themselves of
their deep sadness exhaustion   and want

they believe these dreams are signs of good fishing   the grace of the mighty   ocean
but you know different don't you   that each of your great loves gave a piece of
themselves the night before   so that you three could be alone   have each other
to yourselves   and   only the wind   and the moon know   what really happened
and they'll never tell   except to each other   back and forth   across time

today and long after we are gone   they'll talk about you   and the water the boat
and about   how they provided the atmosphere for such a scandalous breath taking

affair   and if your sons are lucky   one day   they'll hear it   firsthand from you

or maybe   as cornelia   passes into their hands   taking them out onto
the tender sea   your best loves   may with a grieving aching wonder and delight

tell the story   of

how best to love   a man

lena

your death enrages me   but I hear that anger is shorthand for sadness
and so it is that I am sad   the mood   too callous on the occasion of your
neverbeinghereagain those piercing *whataretheycalled* colored eyes

casting nets out into the audience I can believe that hollywood never knew
what to do with you   almost colored *nearlywhite* redbone girl   you had one
nerve opening your mouth to sing   wide mouthed   all red lipped from
what felt like   cupid's bow to tonsil   perfect white teeth

everything about you   a controlled and concentrated venom

not a hair out of place   the depth of your *cradlegivensass* a hiss crackle
sound like charcoal and fire   restrained itself in order for you to become that
moment in time   I remember seeing you   as a child in black and white repeats

on late night   or anytime tv   your bodice and hips   teasingly articulating   themselves

as fine whispers   making people   pretend that they are seeing what they were
seeing   not feeling a hint of love   for the black goddess that stood before them

live and in color

you were this way always   serious and controlled   the smartest one in the room
eager to leave   when you had had enough   of the game of a man of a situation

but always you exited   with a quiet   that left everyone a little more empty
and thread bare   you left willingly polite   and without a bother   as if you had meant

to do just that   at that moment   and for that reason

I deeply resent them you know   these absentminded   starlets skimping
and strutting themselves about   believing   that they are entitled to the songs
they sing   and that they   are not insults to the very nature *of nature*   and what are we

if not tragic buffoons   who belly up to their special brand of madness   fraught
with wardrobe malfunctions   hair weaves and watching them getting their
asses kicked by their boyfriends   and they never know why   and everything is always
beyond their control   and understanding

and we are a little sadder   for having had the experience   live and in color

there is still   so much about you   that is unsung and unsaid   everything is dimmer now
I remember you   but even more of them   remember nothing   and if you are lost to
them what of me   and my memory   and those who believe they will *always* remember me

and now I understand   what the dream meant   many months before you died
you and billie   josephine and dorothy   all of you   good and dolled up

seated at a well done table   the music of your time a backdrop   and how you laughed
while fine men in tuxedos   asked for your hands   across champagne bottles and
nearfilledglasses   and cracked crab plates nodding towards a dance floor filled with people

you were trying to tell me   you were going   that all of you   were okay   and to make sure

whatever I did   to get the story right to tell it honest and true nothing sad and sappy

only this   make you   gracious
beyond belief

and live and in color

tyler perry would love this

I love beauty shops
the poor woman's therapy

a room filled with makeshift divas   both male and female
elbow deep in relaxers hair dye   naturals   box braids

and natty dreds   if you like

some old r&b station plays the tune of the day

today   it is *before I let go*   by frankie beverly
we all know this one

an oldie a goodie   feels like forever
our uniform voices erupt   singing the chorus   together

it is a familial moment from within our DNA that transcends
oceans   slaves ships   and cotton fields   it is what we do

it is this shared moment that has interrupted our conversation
about *our* president

godwelovehim

will take him
the myth and the might of him

and how did we get on this subject
oh   yes   my *obama for your mama*   t-shirt

and someone said   *I love that*
which turned into
I love him
a segue into   *Ilovethewayhelovesmichelle*

each of us nodding   and needing for that love to be real
not political speak or pretend
for what would it do to us   if he were just another man

destined to embarrass her

as she stood disheveled   before the cameras and journalists
mouthing a redundancy *I support my husband ours is a private matter*

but underneath   wouldn't it be those now famous arched eyebrows   signifying
I sacrificed my soul for this man   and all I got was a lousy campaign t-shirt

and where   would we all go from there

but this was not the true matter at hand
not why we were all there   it never is

it is not why so much attention is paid to detail
the right radio station   stylist   clientele

the purpose of the beauty shop is to signify about the human heart

how sacrosanct   how easily breakable

it is why we pay ungodly amounts of money
waiting for hours   losing entire days from our lives   that we will never recover
simply to be placed into someone else's   tender loving care

it is done that we may listen   and be listened to

and so it is a discussion   about a very public love   that sets the stage
for what is to come

my own dreds newly twisted   I sit   needing to stay a little longer
sensing   something

my loctician   has her hands folded in the next client's mane

a black man
nervously fingering his wedding band
sliding it up and down the length of his fingers

clearly uncomfortable with us

too many women   too many black women
too many gay black men   or   maybe   simply worried about the
kind of man he was

I slowly *pretend count* the bills in my hand   until I hear camille say

how's ya man girl and she doesn't miss a beat

still chewing   popping her gum   easing out the words   in what I know to be
the best and most comforting *trini* accent ever

still folding his hair   between her fingers
mouth   full of beautiful white teeth   she waits patiently for an answer

the shop falls silent
for she is a god making a pronouncement
every word a form of caribbean wisdom

he is fine I say *we are fine* I add   with a smile   and genuine contentment
because that is what she really wanted to know

what they all wanted to know
and were readied with true counsel had I needed it

for we are fighting a losing battle   with men these days
partly of our own making   so broke and broke down

the building blocks of our lives   cemented with the memories of the men
who were not good to us
who did not validate us   seemed so very   unsatisfied with us

which in turn   made us so very unsatisfied with   ourselves

she searched my eyes looking for any hint of an untruth in my answer   and
finding none says   *well honey   that is a good thing*

and the amen choir began their chorus
each with a story about how good it is   to be loved   when you've wanted it for so long
or got good and loved   any ole' way   even though you made him pay
so very dearly for the privilege   these love stories are the hardest to bear

why are you here we seem to say   defying these men to love us
what could you want from me   when there is nothing here of value

this woman space literally humming in that moment   is this way   often

keep him happy girl   they tease   winking and back slapping
and I know what they mean   for they are often both irreverent and wise

and the conversation shifts again to the joys of sex

there is such laughter
and   as I pay my bill
it is the man that I notice now
no longer twisting his wedding band   not judging us

nor fearful of us

or of the woman waiting for him at home

he seems almost confident in his ability to love her   past her pain
or at least in his ability to try

and I know   when he enters   the house tonight

dreds soft   scented with lemon grass   hair touched by the hands of another woman
in the holiest of ways   as if offering a prayer for their future

his beloved   will feel something new and redefined within him
because he was battled tested today   and not found wanting

and just maybe   she will let him   hold her   a little bit   tighter

tennessee

because   inside of this skin I am but a little brown girl

I understand the magnitude   the deep down bone chill
you must have felt in the moment

it isn't easy being called out of your name
feels   a lot like leaving the space time continuum

for me   it was a moment of feigned friendship

a delight   in a stolen shake of time   two little girls at play
one white   the other not

imagine my surprise when I learned that you catch niggers   instead of little piggies
never imagined that eaney meanie miney moe   required head gear
knee pads   or that a child be made of tougher stock

I wish   I could have been more brave   in the moment

envied you your fortitude   if not your courage   then at least your gumption
sense of entitlement   the certainty about your humanity

I imagine that in the dark of night   on an endless road   lanterns
and sheet covered people   giving chase
or even during the audacity of a sunlit street

fag sounds like *nigger*   just the same

and as your friends   now pulling at your shirttails bid you to   *turn 'round tennessee*
flee this place   and your lover's tender cry called ahead   *come where you are wanted*
let us run and hide   fall desperately into one another's arms

surely you wanted these things instead   of this
yet another attack on your manhood
wanted instead   your lover's hair   tussled in the pre-dawn light
his easy sly grin   filled with knowing   all the words you'd ever write
dancing along his skin

but instead   tearing away from this vision   and away from their pleas

you   found instead   yet another new form of courage

answering these men   your brothers on any other day   had they been their better selves
your answer   a simple caution

my name is tennessee williams   and I am not in the habit of retreat

and how else could a gay man assert his manhood
but by insisting upon it   and then be willing to lay down his life

to defend himself   in all of the ways that a straight man does

and then be willing to do more

so let that be your epitaph

not that you wrote
nor that you dared to love another man in the light
when it was unfathomable to do so

but that you feared

but loved the freedom of defiance   even more

inaugural: what we've been trying to say since then

barack obama

we are not the bones of our corrupted past
grinding together the spines and vertebrae   of our dreams
down   into a fine paste   meant to build the delights of others

I want to believe instead   that we are this
that always there could have been you

lately   I've been filled with forgiveness
a forgetfulness about past hurts

I'm forgetting about the hunger I felt while waiting at my *father's* table
for his scraps   his acknowledgement   to at least be sent to my room
to even have a room   in his house

a bastard child   is still someone's child   and it wants to be loved

maybe that's what we've been saying   for these several hundred years
we have no other home but this   and we want   to come inside

less and less   I've wanted to be   an imagined   an   invented african

and more and more   I wish to be this   with you
an understood   an assertion   not a question mark
but worthy   isn't that how you see things

I know it was hard   it had to be

I believe   that in the harsh and cold darkness   of   hotel room   after hotel room

when prying eyes   could not see
you put off your easy   toothy grin   swallowed your rage   and cried

because a man is after all a man   and men cry alone in the dark

it is what we allow

for to reveal the depth of your massive sadness   would have made you shed your yoke
who knew if we deserved it   would welcome this new freedom   unstained view of ourselves
what if we destroyed you   just as passionately as we laid ourselves before you

it is the nature of man   to defile what it needs   so desparately

42

ask any who came before you...
what did it take   to shake the hand of stranger after stranger
never knowing   if a handshake   was a bullet

what god did you rely upon
when you heard about the letters   threatening to defile your daughters

how many black men   have had to wade through that inky specter

did you shake your head   when the vultures picked   apart your wife
parsing her words   re-sculpting her face   and the arch of those infamous eyebrows

because she looked angry   like some *angryneckrolling* black woman

maybe   she had cause to be angry   because you couldn't be

no black man who wants something   can afford to be angry
appear vengeful   to be on a mission   be misinterpreted

it's a dangerous world out there   for you   for all of us

were you thinking all of this   pillow over your face
stilling the great goliath   the madness surely to unfurl   had you cried out
like jesus on the cross   *am I to be forsaken*

who knows if we even deserve you

maybe it's shameful that so much depends upon you
but every god   of every generation needs a prophet

every prophet must lead   even when they are flawed   scared
or are wanting to be something else
anything   other than what they are

I wish you a better people   that's supposed to be the evolution of things
we're supposed to age and strengthen   throughout the annals of time
know more   do better   renew old friendships   heal old historical hurts

and it isn't necessarily you   that I wish to be worthy of   but   rather   the moment
for the time   when I am as much a promise for you   as you are for me

I wish you a messiah all your own   a moses   to part the waters for you
a mary to wipe your tears   because you should be free to shed them
we've all needed these things   why else brave the hulls of ships
auction blocks   hooded faces   and the heavy boughs of trees   bearing their strange fruit

but I think we need more now   more than the pain to sustain us
more than a dream

much more than a promise

and I don't know what we will find out   about ourselves now
as a race
as a nation

but won't it be something   if we get there together

mean mugging

today   you are my problem   but I just know
tomorrow   you are destined   to become someone else's

and shame on me for saying it   for seeing it in a child
who barely knows how to tie his own shoe
but I see in you   now   what I fear every day   on the streets

on the streets   the other day   I saw a man   small in stature
body held tight   a firm stance   determined gait
eyes burrowing into the back before him   I guess we've become accustomed
to this kind of everyday   *bodyspeak*   as new yorkers

as new yorkers   our body language signals   to the fellow sojourners   who walk beside us
I am not to be fucked with   but it was too early in the morning
to be this determined   this resistant   to humanity   but   nevertheless   there he was
and   had I not felt compelled to look on further   I would have missed
entirely   that he was actually   a child

a child   so filled with cruelty   malice   contempt hissing from his body
toward the audacity of the morning hour   his mother tugging at his   bicep
pushpulling him across the city street   her own fatigue and mental   *whywhywhy*
of her life edging her on   scowl on her face   and this child   I'm sure   will have   a bad day

a bad day   is in store for all who come before   this child   and   why not
when the   last words   spoken on the doorstep of his school are
I'm hungry   and she replied   *too gotdamn bad   just get away from me*
it is the stuff of   made-for-tv dramas
I waited for the music   the signal for a scene change   to accompany her abrupt
shift of weight   as she turned on her heels   entered the subway   and I followed behind
wondering what happens to   such a child

such a child   is everywhere before me these days   on days
when the world is very much with me   or when I am one with it
and while my own moods ebb and flow   theirs never appear to   at all
an encounter with a child these days   is a decision   a question   that you must be ready
to ask of yourself   *the morgue or jail*   in exchange for your self-respect as an adult

as an adult   it shouldn't be this way   I should read for pleasure or escapism
on a city bus or train   not out of fear of making eye contact   with a young life
wishing to crash into my own   because it has to   in order to prove a point
to me   the other passengers   or the co-conspirators   at his or her side   mugging
for the invisible cameras   that film and follow their lives

their lives will mean something   later that night   at the expense of
someone else's peace of mind   and the sun will set on the mayhem   of the previous day
and they will sleep through whatever truly grieves their soul   rise to crush another day
pretending it hasn't already broken them   wanting someone in the house
that should be at home   to   give   a   damn

give   a   damn I want to say to my neighbor who will not control her son
does not seem to understand that parenting is not a suggestion that mothers
who do not put their foot down will soon find what's left of their child
underneath someone else's   and I want to be better than the cycle
that predestines this child   to what I feel is inevitable   but I know no other
defense to this illness that pits our children   against us

nothing but their fear   that has now cooled crystalized   and become my very own

unnatural disasters

call back the waters

I.
Baptism

we brought you home   placed you in the bassinet
stood over you and waited   for you to become something
your father made caring for you   almost ritualistic

eager to meet your needs   you were practically never wet
nor given time to cry   to indicate   that you were hungry
such a whirlwind   to appease you   to make you succinct
appropriate for the world

it seemed best to stand on the wayside of your life   waiting for the subterranean
deep earth   to shift inside me   for only that   it seems   could make me   want me
want you   and as the priest dipped your body in the baptismal fount

still   I felt nothing   no tugging at my breast as your diminutive frame
called out to me   wanting to be fed   held close

and I   said this to the priest   later   as the days gave way to weeks
giving way to months   that there was nothing   where my heart should be
nothing but the mounting pressure to want to you   when it seems
that everyone did   except me

the man who shares my bed   eager to do yet another grandiose thing
that asserts his right to be ruler of the world   master of my body
entitled to the mound between his thighs

a gynecologist waving his *tictoc* finger at me   warning against women
waiting too long   to do   what they were first born to do
his mother   my mother   other mothers   everyone   wanting uniformity
a sameness in an effort to keep   the inane game going

maybe   people expect too much good from a woman   and never seem to believe
that a mother can have dark hands   ignoring that this skip in natural mother love
isn't always the baby blues but   dread   the body soul   and mind

resisting what is *un-natural* to it

faced with too much shame   and never enough time
for anyone to bear witness no mercy no grace   for a mother who feels this way
something   otherly   it seems   crisscrossed   the wires in my head   closed me off

to the rational and because there would never be   any grace   no tender mercy
on my behalf   I learned to shut my mouth   pretend   cajole and smile
because it is expected   preferred   best   just to keep the game going
no one wanted to know   to raise an eyebrow question my character
for what would that mean about what we think we know

and I wonder what god would do this bring you to me allow this
to hang before me   like low fruit on a dead tree

and I swear to you   I intended this for me designed a good death for myself
the water unbearably hot   to scald   perhaps to burn out the demon

but you cried and I did not hear the voice of god and good reason   but
instead you wanting yet again what I could not give
a place to fall softly in this hard world

mercy   I shouted out to no one in particular   feeling the stillness of your now
gone-away body   and the sting of the water on my hands unknown to me now

skin peeling away it too rejecting me   they will know now   I believe   to never trust
take an absolute for granted   understand that there are demons in all of us

that we may all   very well be god's children   but wouldn't you know it
the devil   has just as many

II.
Katrina

perhaps if they had given you a different name I would have taken heed
believed you capable of grave harm and carnage   but they called you something tender

at times   painted you   as a coy woman   prone to changing your mind
heading off in a different direction   as it is a woman's prerogative to do

and   because we do not take women seriously   I found nothing lasting
or sustainable in you   no threat   and looked only for the limitations of your promise

but   like any good mother I dressed my twins   and kept them close
placed our *togobag* by the door   had we needed to make a hasty departure

I was smug self-congratulatory   proud   that I had not aborted my children
when their souls entered my body   was steadfast   when their father would not be
owning up to that fact   that I had not made better choices
but would spend the rest of their lives making up for my reckless youth

I was comforted by our tiny home   paid for with my own money   satisfied
that I could come home to them with clean hands
having stood on my feet   serving others instead of   offering up my flesh   to men

who didn't care that I was someone's mother   perhaps even aroused by it
sensing   need and desperation a willingness to do more   and walk away with less

I could have done it   raised two black sons   grown them into men   without souring
them on women or turning them into momma's boys   forging them into the
replacement   for the emptiness of my own bed

but   I turned my back on happenstance   remembered too late   what I marveled at
in every tale I ever read in greek mythology   that the gods find our peace
and certainty loathsome   will do almost anything to take away our happiness

and it seems that the fates use their scissors when drunk
or bored   finding humanity tedious

had zeus looked down   found me appealing in some odd way   raised an eyebrow
and his sin became my own   my penance to be brought low   washed away

to appease the broken heart of a goddess

and gladly   I would have given my life
endured a thousand different tortures   to spare my children

my children one on either side of me   safe in our bed   we fell asleep listening to
the sound of the rain   then just a storm   and   in a moment   something
so altogether different   much stronger than my wit and drive

and the first floor   surrendered to the waters   and our roof gave our bodies
to the tree   that sat alongside our home

I couldn't hold them both and keep us all safe
and I understood then   that this was my true punishment

for whatever my offense   to meet the proverbial fork in the road
find out   what I was truly made of

to understand that man is very much like the gods   can both do and imagine
the unfathomable   can indeed   split a baby   down the middle

I let my left hand slip   using my now free arm to

climb higher still   my own tears and wailing   now   part of the

surrounding maelstrom   my surviving child grieving   for what it had lost
unsure of whether or not to be grateful for its life

or frightened by what I would do to preserve it

and while waiting   held up by fate   and the unwillingness of the
toosoakedbranches   to lose any more   that day   to the tide

I vowed to never be so certain again

to trust nothing   not my love   anyone else's   or the actions of my own hands

III.
black water for lashaundra armstrong

I'm tired   is a very strong statement   even worse when seconded   by *I've had enough*
but   to be   followed up by   *I've made a mistake*   all within a twenty-four hour
period   a good and mighty *splitsecond*   well over   the cliff   of your life

when you will   never make a bad decision again   and it's too late to adjust   the worst
one ever   is much too much   for anyone to bear   and tomorrow   I will wake up dead

and fuck me for trying   no one   not no one   ever tells you   that it is going to be like this
that every child does not come   into this world   hoping   free and full of promise

I have been a lifetime of damage   bone deep to the molecules   and have taken
these children   with me   and how and why   do they get born   with a wide universe
knowing   I will do   such a thing

there is no god   there just can't be   why wouldn't he rewind   this blaspheming
nightmare   couldn't this   seeping wet   making its way through   sole of shoe and
stockinged winter feet   pant-leg   crotch   and the wretched frigidness   of our

scaled tomb   be instead   a wet dream   find me maybe   in my bed   finger clenching
the sheets   re-living the night I conceived   these children   I'd settle   for a night terror
that I am imagining this   vile trauma   and have yet to go this far

let me awake   matted   hair   t-shirt nighty   soggy and clinging to me   bed linen strewn
about the floor   panic   crunched down   into a deep red ball in my throat

and the water   is the still dreaming sweat   between my toes   squishing down
in the carpet fibers   as I   on tip toe   exit the bedroom   searching and listening
clammy fingertips   before me on the walls   in the darkness   edging me along

until I find each child in their beds asleep moonlight through the mirror windows
and I can hear each breath laced with a vivid dream about tomorrow
tomorrow tomorrow another sunrise some ridiculous doll
or video game of the month silly song sung by another silly singer
flavor of year years upon years of *she's bothering me get out of my room
you make me sick* graduations first menstrual blood condom and birth control talks
scholastic aptitude tests college and weddings sweet joy such a sweet fanciful joy

all this you get from the miracle of lying down and letting someone enter your body
and take with them a piece of your spirit a wet kiss thirsty and long all this
the bride price of love

but not before the countless air and sound barrier piercing cries of mommmmy…
unlike anything you've ever heard before it is a sternum-opening wound to a caring mother
finding a skinned knee broken arm hurt feeling or a child who just wants to know that
you are close by not far just mommy mommy who is close ever so close by

I have done wrong here I know now yanked back from a wish that will never be
mommy isn't safe mommy is too close tragic tomorrow morning's news

and it's *why mommy mommy please* that has my terrified futile hands clenching
at buttons and levers believing what that car salesman said about driving in reverse

I have done this thing delivered them to and from water and here on the edge
of losing everything and my faith god is a little boy stronger than me

one sweeping act of grace left in me hands on his pantlegs praying he knows
that I am not holding him back but it is me yesterday's me urging him forward

and do you hear me son *mommy was wrong*

little girls...

the trouble with little girls is   that they are often unwanted   biblically inferior
exported   by way of dowries   or international adoptions
subject to mutilation   and are often   somebody's garbage can kids

renamed   as we pass through the hands of men
what are we to make of ourselves   as women
when first we are constructed   and framed by the eyes of males
when we are but   little girls

what then is a woman to herself

perhaps   she is the child within
on guard   waiting to be noticed   given an opinion
learning how to run the gauntlet of a man's world   from the women in her life

who learned the rules   from the women in theirs

what is it they say about circles and their vicious nature
we've made women into circles   their natures' vicious
into   a hard thing

maybe there is no danger in men   but the power we give them

and a woman is the anvil about her own neck   and that of her sisters and daughters
while the patriarchal shift is   the price we've paid because we want them

more than we want us

tell me   when is a daughter   ever her mother's enemy

on a walk   through a mall   because that's what we women do   when we're not *gossiping*
we walk through malls   looking for the perfect purchase to change us
further un-complicate us   we walk through the bar-less cage   looking
often in the company of other women   namely our daughters

looking   and   hurting
and
well
you know   hurt people   hurt people

and I find this mother   this daughter
both dressed in the fashion of the day

so much so   that one is indistinguishable from the other
because   in this new-fangled world   mothers and daughters would rather be   sisters
and what care we for our sisters
what is she   but a threat   an obstacle   competition

but   had we mothers   real mothers   *yesterday*   kinds of mothers   who tend
to show up in our yesteryear melodies   that trigger   *yes* feelings   pulling at
everything until there is nothing left   but the raw agony of being first and best
loved unconditionally   we would then know   what the cantor means when he says

sadie sweet sadie   don't you know we love you sweet sadie or
I'll always love my momma cause she's my baby girl

only these kinds of mothers could teach us better   about the worth of our sisters
and how best to care for them

and yet   here before me   not mother not daughter   but sisters

and the pretend mother looks upon her daughter   filled with disdain and regret
anger and frustration   and a belly full of want and longing

and well   hurt people hurt people

what the fuck is wrong with you   she says
everyday it's the same shit with you   she says
you never do anything right

and the daughter is puzzled   because minutes before
in this bizarro world they were sisters   *gurls*

then   the daughter slides the stolen backpack   down along her spine
forcing the mother to slide her own stolen goods   along the length of her arm

this is what sisters teach one another

I am so sick of you this mother says

they are both scared now
both under the gaze of men with power

do they run   pretend   put on that bad girl pluck that we're prone to
when the world has eaten away at all of our armor

they leave a mother wanting   a daughter dazed   confused
punch struck as if having gone the distance with Ali

the question *why doesn't she love me*   huge   hanging in the air above us in this
bar-less cage   had we all heard it   surely we would have dropped to our knees in prayer
as women are often called to do   pray in the face of hopelessness

and perhaps I could have understood the mayhem
had the bags been filled with food   sanitary napkins   or cotton underwear

but who sells a daughter's esteem for a school backpack   two designer handbags
and three pairs of   low rider jeans

I remember dancing this dance with my own mother
thinking I was the false face on the daughter   she should have had
just a brooklyn hood girl   who was never supposed to be more than a hood rat

looking up into the screaming   scalding   berating face
the clenched and swinging fists of my own mother

I wondered   why   I guess she wanted   needed to be my sister
because   being my mother meant   that her time
had come   and gone

my birth signaled her lost opportunity   and by god   didn't I see   she seemed to be telling me
through her own tears   and the unfathomable darkness of her hurt   my god
why couldn't I see   that she had nothing of value to give me   but her own hurt

maybe mothers give their daughters   their hurt   because in the place of our real power

our hurt   is the only thing as equally powerful   as our joy
it is the black angel that drives us up   and through evil   and so they give us this
but it is a poor   insufficient substitute

and like the memory of any bad deed   we have ever done
it echoes
and lies
like the demons of mental illness to a potential suicide   recklessly
and un-cautioned it whispers

you have to take what you want

and that's what   the mother in the mall meant   between insults

you have to take what you want   nothing is given   not nothin'

nothin'
is free

take it   even if you have to take it from me sister

chi-town

I.

JJ   Thelma and Michael
made it out of the ghetto

it is the stuff of   *I told you so*   dreams

and they did it all by themselves   too
with the pens of talented writers   and
the ever-fine production skills of mr norman lear

and what an exit

daddy didn't leave in the middle of the night
he wasn't a pimp a hustler   a batterer   or even
a dope-dealing   black man on the grind

he died at the wheel   on his way back to the family
having carved out a new life for them   elsewhere…

Florida held it together as black women are apt to do
and JJ stopped acting like a fool
learned how to make a black body on canvas   palatable

Michael went to college   Thelma married a football player
who only hit her   once

and they left us
bringing their sassy black neighbor Wilona along with them
and wasn't it great when they let Janet Jackson
go along for the ride

and we   were so proud

when the Evans' morphed into the Jeffersons
leaving the north side of Chi-Town for   the east side
of Park Avenue in NYC

and I can tell you   George never hit Weazy

and we thought ourselves safe

when the Chicago deciders   blew to bits
the cinder block door frames and moldings
of so many housing developments

go   they seemed to say
infiltrate assimilate
impose yourself elsewhere

the Evans' don't live here anymore
George and Weazy are senior citizens
and Lionel will inherit an empire

II.

I understand now   how black folk came to nickname
housing developments   the projects

they   with just a simple phrase   where able to encapsulate
what it really means to be   poor   uneducated
compromised   out of choices and   black

it is   quite simply   a project

you see   beyond black pride   and civil rights and the
strong educated powerful black woman   it must be said

that a good portion
of black folk   despise each other
because black skin   it is quite simply   a project

shackling ourselves to gang warfare
making it impossible to leave your project without
tilting your hat this way or that   in order to keep from getting shot
or hassled   until the next day

and   like all weak-kneed bullies
afraid   someone will actually make it out   get away
have a story to tell   that doesn't involve basketball   drugs   or hip hop music

they hold entire   communities hostage
taking aim at mothers walking babies to school
fathers who dared to remain with their families
coming home on the late shift   men just like James Evans

or that one young boy   barely a man
whose father drove him to school   every day of his life
until he graduated   so that he would never have to   tilt his hat
choose between   being a scavenger or a predator

and they shot him dead   in front of his church
after he entered the night air   easy smile on his face

shot dead   weeks from the safety   of a far away college classroom
guitar in his hand   a musician in the church choir

a drive-by for no reason   aimless and random
he died   on the sidewalk   and daddy wasn't there
because he should have been   safe at church

that's what his mother said   clutching his guitar case

she asked the CNN anchor *why wasn't my baby safe   at church*

and nobody saw nothin'   gripped by fear   complicit
in our own purposeful demise   held hostage by the fathers
who had the audacity   to abandon   us

our best is a jail cell   being someone's baby mama

these days   being black is quite simply   a   project

III.

and so now   here we are

the north side   west side   and south
converging upon that proverbial fork in the road

once separate   mutually understanding
where the other   did   and did not belong

they have no choice now

the b boys   baby mommas
future b boys and baby mommas
see little difference between themselves
and the *black other* the   *made it out* others

and they pass by   uninhibited
threatened and threatening

until   a made it out of the ghetto   black man
maybe James Evans   angered that he now has to live next to
what he left behind   dares   lift his voice   in protest   from the window
of his five bedroom   three bathroom
two guest room having house   in the highlands

just around the corner from Jessie Jackson

in frustration   he shouts to the boys   that could have easily been
JJ or Michael   had they not gotten out

will you ignorant   black niggers   get from in front of   my house

it is a certain death knell
as the young men motion   toward fingers   made into guns

and we all understand how this will play out
anyone who watches
Chicago news   knows how *this* will play out

it is the end of the age of innocence in Chi-Town
worlds are converging
fates have been decided

and everyone   knows that the world
will surely   end

this time 'round

sak pasé

(hatian patois for "what's up?")

how very sad   it must be   to be   always moving
weightless   in a world of gravity   rootless   although
you've found a place to set up shop

but   who are   we kidding   it has always been temporary

scooped up   one day   so many yesterdays ago
almost an eternity   if you're into history and time
and what they   echo to us   about ourselves
on the eve   of a new day   or during the un-forgivable
stillness   of a   too silent twilight

it wasn't any easier *then*   tied ankle to arm   belly to back
foreign tongue to deaf ear   a sea of black skin   now rolling
on the sea   delivering us god knows where

but you must stand   wherever you are

like a sapling in a new soil   you must take root   or die

make a home   where there is none   and your name is a non-issue
and so is your body   or anything you ever knew about yourself

and so you learn to be new   chattel even   accepting of the
misfortune   until an unfolding within you   tells you   you are not
this damned and damaged thing
you've heard about   in the place of your own true name

and so you learn to be   a dissident   a hell-raiser
until you become free   wondering still of your people   across the pond
or on the shores of the not too far away islands
where the cruelty of the sandy beaches   and *tooblue* water   lie to you

stirring something within you   that reads almost like home
and so you learn to become   something new there too

only to find in a generation   or a blink of an eye   that indeed
there is no new thing under the sun
and that in the place   of the hunger for ancestral memory
your new pangs   very real and substantial   are in your very own belly

and   in that of your children   and now   the enemy is the hunger
and want   in your neighbors' eyes

my god you must be thinking   *when we were chattel   at least we were fed*

and now this final insult to your injuries   no boats   no guns
torches ablaze   or white sheets giving chase   or tree branches
swinging low   with the strange fruit   that is   your kin

it is   instead   the very earth   this time around   a grave moaning
from its very bowels that assaults   what is left of your soul

and how do you explain this new evil

hold on   to logic   or to the remains of your sanity

to be chased from your bed   in the early morning hour   out onto your
already destitute streets   a vagabond   even to the earth

and what new   what   fresh hell is this   why are we so unwanted
fair so unwell no matter the hue   or dialect

or   maybe   my thoughts grow   too dark at this hour
unable to see that there is a way out of egypt
a wisdom   in not   splitting the baby down the middle

and   instead   the huge up-ending   of yet another portion
of our storm cloud ridden   inky world   was a knell   pulling at something

long dormant   meant to gather the children   splintered and scattered about

the earth   maybe meant to guide us to the great meeting place

where we'll stand on the shores   of this *brokeninhalf* world
until yet another great wave

sweeps up her lost children   and carries them altogether   home

to see the world

the harsh truth is *destiny*   the television doctor said   to the viewing audience
as they often do   launching new specters into the universe   as if there isn't
enough to fear these days   the economy   birthers   *blackmeninwhitehouses*

but apparently   there is yet another unknown   a great terrific masquerading
behind our deep sadness   edging us toward something more

quite common *he says* for the creative citizens of our world to suffer from
a deep melancholy   the writers   painters   singers   true artists
suffer to put forth their very own vision of the world   and also because of what they see

it would seem   some form of your sanity   is the final blood price to meet the world as it is
or as it is meant to be   and what are we to do with that

when the *singsong* voices in your head tell you   that   *we* are all we need

how to place that kind of information on the canvas   to will the color palette into
becoming something more than it is in one ephemeral moment   be both ordered and free

how best to sing or shake loose the body   in an effort to convey the same meaning

that man is a god   with good intentions   but capable of so much harm

how best to live inside this world   when the give and take of   surrendering
to whatever your art is the uncertainty   of yourself alone   behind the wheel of a car
face to face with your children   or   in your lover's   arms

and I don't mean silly starlet behavior either   stepping out of limousines with a bare crotch
middle finger to world   commonplace drug addiction   as if a stage you pass through

on the way to a grammy an oscar   or a best-selling autobiography

I mean the *downdeep* hurtful darkness of a muse   who pursues its host with a vengeance
calling the writer   like a siren   upon the jagged rocks of a generation

a writer who understands   not her grief or from where this *pushpulling* of events comes

but instead   knows somehow that there must be words down on the paper
upon the walls   in the corners of the attic   with the blood of her hands   if need be

how best to love someone who loves the world so much   they cannot fathom themselves

or   to watch them sketch   the formaldehyde dead body of their baby   or the corpse
of a lover   blow out the blue flames of a gas oven   with their children in
the next room   slice skin   endure the misunderstood eternal rage
a battle with god himself   it isn't a gift   always   and is

sometimes   a burden   to see the world   know it tenderly
with an intimate touch   to hear it call to you   with a clouded bitter sweetness

knowing   what it means   instead   to be caught between

this world   and the next

unsteady

unsteady

"you go girl"
the graffiti on the wall said
and it wasn't a note of encouragement either

was not placed in its proper context

said between girlfriends
or man to woman   when no other words would suffice

was not an awkward expected punchline on a sitcom

instead
rather
this way   on a brooklyn wall
the phrase felt like an accusation   an indictment

deep disappointment

seemed to be saying   instead
where are you going girl   and why aren't you there yet

I've been feeling a little unsteady lately
watching thirty something turn into yet another thirty something
feeling as   un-empowered as ever

it turns out   that all of the slogans we were told as girls   as women

were quite wrong

we have not come a long way baby
it does not look good on us
people do not always think   we are worth it
things are not easy or breezy   we are not covergirls

even hearing   I love you is sometimes a shady prospect   at best
and don't get me started on happily ever after…

our mothers neglected to tell us what life is really like
that it is actually *after* us

is not interested in us or the slogans   we bear   like tattoos along the body

turns out   that a woman was never meant to be   a catchy signature phrase

she is too deep a chasm
delightfully unknown   even to herself   in many ways

and I wonder
why it is   that I should be made to understand myself so completely   just now

when nothing fashioned by the divine hand of the gods
or from within the big bang of the universe
knows me at all

maybe that is the lot of women
to be made stationary and confused by those who could never comprehend us

the old stories of creation   say to us   eat this and bear the sin of man
be silent   bring forth the son of god
but do not look back   to see what god hath wrought   or else be made into stone

know nothing   stand still   bear witness
to the ensuing madness

I blame god for the conundrum
for the hardness of trying to figure it all out

but   maybe

there is still time to praise and be praised
to feel divine   and make divinations

regenerate like the cells of the body

and I think back to those words

cemented into the fabric of the city   that I love
that is so much like a woman

dense   sacred   white hot to the touch

what it must have taken to scale the wall
equipped only with a can of brown spray paint

daring the streets to acknowledge her presence

knowing that she would never build a bridge

that her name would never appear on any of the surrounding buildings
that in her city   somewhere
a woman was being dragged into an alley to be violated
still more   were being smashed to bits   in their very own homes
that perhaps one day   her own daughter

as a means of so-called rebellion
in the house where she paid the mortgage   and kept the lights on

that daughter would slam a door   and with great nerve and certainty
scream *I hate you*

maybe these words were for them   as much as they were for herself
that day   maybe they were   for me

who needs them so much these days
when I'm feeling so deeply   unsteady

needing to be brave   and masterful
bigger in imagination and wit   than my own body

and I'm grateful for her unselfishness   the manifesto
the gentle uncomplicated love poem
and I'm thinking   if she could be bothered to write them

shouldn't I be brave enough to live them

brooklyn state of mind: the caterpillar poem

I.

how you doing girlfriend   Ming says to me   as I enter the laundry

as usual   I have waited   until my underwear drawer
is down to two pair of panties   and one good bra   it is shameful

but life   and my mind   are crowded   heavy with other things   these days
like the passage of time   and making love   and thinking about the passage
of time   and making love

these are the kinds of things   that keep you from doing your laundry

when you begin to see yourself   as you really are   not as a fixed thing

and you come to understand   that forward movement   is a blessing
necessary   for your own survival   that all things must move

like your body   no longer twenty   not even thirty   but a comfortable
thirty something marveling at how welcome   and well suited you are
in your own hips   in the morning   looking down upon him   your hands on his body

his upon yours the sweet scent of sex and sweat tasting like salt and sugar
morning sun   an added highlight   dancing through the blinds   playing peek-a-boo
along the sheets and his skin

and you know that time   has taught you   that loving   and being loved
are skills that must become   an art form
which is so necessary   for your own survival

or your neighborhood   your very own   since you were but a child   ever a mosaic

once flavored with a pantheon of brown and black faces   laid beautifully
against a brooklyn skyline   with a sole lone white neighbor   who found black
to be ever beautiful   home in every way

a neighbor who loved the promise of standing still so much
that he moved   when both the faces and races
of his beloved home   began to morph into an unknown

I too remember being terrified   about what it would all mean   feeling new
in my own space considered an unknown quantity to a fresh pair of eyes so unlike my own

but to keep what has always been so certain   to me
just who would I   be inclined to surrender

Ming   who I am almost positive   is learning all of her english   from re-runs
of *living single*   or some other such   used to be   all black sitcom

her father   who greets every b-boy   who enters   with a dap and a soul hug

instead of with fear despite that fact   that he has seen them   saunter off
to the nether regions of this alice and wonderland   world of ours
become threatening   hate filled   using that same dap or pound to pass on
their specific brand of death

shall I shake loose from my soul Ira   who holds a passover for all
of his neighbors   despite their otherness

I've grown accustomed to their faces   mesmerized
by the confidence they exude   while striding   this their new world

II.

how commonplace it is now for a blond two-year-old boy to point to the calendar
on the wall of the bodega and say   *look momma president obama*

and every sunday   feels like christmas morning   as the two neighboring
all black churches have a battle royale   between the choirs

voices bleeding into the ether   crisscrossing together the words
to *sacred secret*   and   *the rest of our days*

on days like these even the non believers   come to understand   why some folk need faith

I've grown accustomed to this city's outrageousness   the subway rides
that are a testament to our eternal internal fortitude delivering us   to
workhouses   warehouses   and whorehouses

or to   the lights of broadway or neighborhoods that would just as soon
spit on us than accept us   the willingness to be cast into the hands   or moods of
whoever is driving the train   that day   trusting them to deliver us home again

where we are best needed   and wanted

I know how to live here   whatever the season   these crooked concrete streets
know how best   to love us   the gang member throwin' up his or her signs

the unforgivable bitch on the bus   who is just looking for a reason   the *o.g.* in the wheelchair   still thinking he's big pimpin'

every jew and gentile   every asian   in all of their beautiful dimensions   the bourgeoisie black   who rolls their eyes   at their downtrodden other halves

III.

we learned our lessons   about life   and forward movement   from an insect

I was there I watched it happen   a caterpillar   breaking free   from
the dying womb   of its own body

raging against standing still   against being ordinary
and terrified   in a forward moving world

knowing   that in a sea of whirlwind change you're bound to cross paths
with *jawdroppingcrazy*

that in order to turn sideways and let it pass you

you have   to be willing to give something of yourself   over to
the   unknown and the darkness   that surrounds us

to better balance the world
for everyone

here   we know   what we know   with our whole
complete
and entire heart

how better and more perfectly loved   by the universe
is the life given a chance

to become   something   altogether new

they say this is a love poem too...

the word of the day was nappy

easing from the lips of a white man   behind a microphone
and the world closed its collective check book   a job was lost
the economics of race won out

but there was no truth

because the truth is   that I have been nappy most of my life

before pomade hot combs   silk wraps   and hair weaves

the call of *bring your nappy headed ass in this house*
or *sit your nappy head still*
is a *notsodistant* echo for most brown ears

the truth is   thirteen percent of the american population   bears the birthmark
on the tops of our heads   the folds in between our legs   on the coarse canvas of the body

it is the delightful brand   of blackness
and while it is unacceptable   to ever be a white man's *nappyheadedanything*

where is the collective financial outrage for the platinum front crotch grabbin'
mic in the hands   black men   for whom black women are everything but   sacred

each one of them   pushed into the world   through full lips
surrounded and cushioned   by soft nappy terrain

now men now power brokers over the black woman's anatomy

what then are we   commodified   legs spread   cash spilling over our thongs
while crissy and moet are poured over our bodies   as we sway to a hip hop beat

who am I to this man   am I me   or am I his *muchhated* mother
would he like to take his diamond encrusted fingers...

a ring for every million he's sold
asking me to grab a pole   bend over and touch my toes

...does he want to take that violent hand   ball it into a terrified fist   beat his chest
 mark his territory   to ward off the threatening members of his multi-platinum herd

or   might he just point one of those be-speckled fingers at me
as an accusatory mark of shame

now is the time for truth
we women may be electras   but men are oedipal

and no man   above all hated things   will suffer a whore to live

and while these men grab their music awards
thanking god and their mommas
never daddy   just god   and their mommas…

I'm beginning to think they hate what they love

every story is the same story   born of young black mothers   no fathers
hungry days and nights   mean streets   too many mouths to feed   the need to hustle
the so-called ghetto grind

and I cannot help   but wonder
if this misogynist bravado is a repressed rage against a mother
they believe did not do enough   and made all of the wrong choices

what would those lyrics sound like   within a sturdy hip hop beat
a clear truth   for a broken black man child

these are hard questions to ask

because   as black folk
when we are little   black   *nappyheadedchildren*
we are taught not to question

and we must never break our mother's hearts

we do not ask her where our fathers are   why there are more children in the house
than there is money in her pocket book

and when we are little girls
we do not ask her why she seems to love our brothers more

we do not question her judgment
her burden   seems big enough

and   maybe   this is how we have come to this

exacting a sick revenge on one another

sacrificing the truth of ourselves for food
esteem for a bank account

our good name for a grammy
but the truth is   we better learn to forgive our mothers   and our fathers too
for their un-chastened imprint

the great body of water that shaped and formed us

is also wearing us down

cradle board

for ryan gover-shieldchief

I once wrote a poem for your mother   in it   were spotted horses   cedar   black coffee
reservations songs   and pow wow legends   with cracked leather faces

a broken heart for each of the letters in our names

these are the things one writes of   when you are learning   an indian woman

in the poem we sang yoruba songs   if you can imagine   a homeless
black woman   teaching a pawnee indian   sacred   soft-sounding songs
about   africa   longing and want

an indian woman   who *knows* where she lives   and that anywhere   is her home rightfully

in this two-step world we shawl danced   to cement our friendship   exchanged feathers
cloth and diet coke   on a rock   near a lake in oklahoma   it seems we understood things

content   with the exchange   a good trade   as far as treaties go

we were remnants   dog-eared pages   on the dusty ledger of life
and history   such a fine printed   footnote   we made

but we believed   in power and magic   great catastrophes
and in the martyrdom   of brown women   that the people may live

believing in our respective causes   we audaciously   opened ourselves   to great visions
no mythical dances around   cauldrons   or meetings in the woods with men
to give us our power

some days   your mother dreamed my dreams   seeing herself   in the hull of a
bottomless ship tethered to the living   and in between the dead   on other days
I dreamed hers   was once given   the true name of her god   in my hands

but the greatest vision   I have ever had   was of you in your mother's arms
her illness your life   and some non-descript   young indian man   in the
background   longing to stay

so it's hard to figure   you see   you were a named thing   a certainty   a formed idea
fulfillment of the circle   a line in a pendleton blanket   to wrap around ourselves
on the   loneliest of   blue dawn days

maybe   even an indian princess some future day

you were not a government statistic   making less than ten thousand dollars a year
not a victim of fetal alcohol syndrome   a suicide   *afailuretothrivebaby*

your household did not want   nor wait for government commodities
cans of meat   boxes of pasta   uncleaned   cloudy rice

your belly   would have been filled with breast milk fry bread
and your mother's corn soup

so your mother and I were right   about   brown women brown skin   and death

and we wonder   who you gave your *threedayold* life for   much to the astonishment
of western medicine   western logic   there is still so much they do not know about us
or   even we of ourselves

no one   expected you to leave   maybe a treaty remains unbroken because you lived
because you had a name because someone bound ribbon and stitched you
a cradle board

you lived for three days   and in yoruba you are the daughter of elegua
the road-opener earpiece of god   the one who opens and closes the doors of our lives

to what we want   need   desire

in which case   you have transcended   been lifted up   become more than my niece
a great grand daughter   of the prairie and the desert

maybe

even

a new word   for god

snapped

this   is a very bad idea   and from what great   brain trust
this circumstance of events sprung   forth   I cannot say

to be relegated willingly   to one set of numbers   on the remote control
must have appeared as a divine light in the sky   to some talking head

one who felt empowered   about taking such a supposed stride forward
on behalf of women everywhere

but   this is a bet   we are sure to lose   a gamble with our very integrity
that is bearing down heavy   on the heads of our daughters

and it must be said   there is no there *there*   but a repeat command performance
of the worst of us   our silliness and befuddlement set loose upon the world

as much as I know   I could never have understood
how grave the psychic damage of a woman's universe

it is it seems the place where good women   and their ideas go to die
morphing into stereotypes   that so easily fit a woman's frame

the lovelorn   rejected   up by her own boot straps   cinderella-in-waiting

modern day black face for women   litany of a silly re-run life

we seem all too willing to fall prey to

wrapping ourselves   up in the bed sheets and quilts   fuzzy socks on our feet
box of kleenex   at our side   while the miracle of a televised life
in marathon movie of the week format   shoos us away from
being interested in   our own

and we weep   for each woman   as the man of her dreams
comes out of his coma   back from the dead   or through the portals of time

just to love her   and only her   in a   *very special way*

and how easily we transition toward the darkest embers of a woman's soul

watching   as our sisters take   their oaths in blood over the bodies
of these same men   in real life   and the narrator oozes with great detail

about just what made penelope   fifi   portia or jennifer   move beyond
all good reason   into the abyss of her own   gaping maw of a soul

because she   wanted out   or he wanted more   or the inside fuzziness
of her own brain   did not come with instructions

come monday morning   at work   the *watercoolerspeak*   becomes
a weekend flashback of *did you sees   wasn't it great   I cried till I ran out of tears*

only surpassed by those shed   when carrie finally got   *mr. big* to marry her

and it ought to make the soul sick   that the average woman
wouldn't be caught dead being labeled a feminist but   the poorest
and most abused people   among us   on the planet are women

and we still make less than men   and while hillary   nearly became president
we are   for the most part   nurses teachers and secretaries

and there wouldn't be anything wrong with that
except not nearly enough people   expect us   to be anything more

and while the militia in *nearlydying   upfromtheashes* countries
on this side of the world   or that   steal children and rape the women

and fathers slip into their sleeping daughters' beds at night
shaving their locs to be traded   so that the starlet of the hour
or one of the *real* housewives of atlanta   orange county   or new york
can rock flowing tresses

still more of our sisters   line the halls of shelters because
staying out of his way   became a next to impossible feat

in this that should be our glorious shining time our daughters look to us
and   find nothing useful   and why would they

we are not nearly as alluring   as life on reality tv   one more step into a contrived
allreadywritten   personality   as if push-up bras   false eyelashes
and the casting couch   weren't enough

who would want to be a *real* woman
when you can be fantastic   lie lazy   in someone else's design

maybe we are indeed   all trapped in the matrix   prefer the coded life played out
before us   while our minds and bodies happily atrophy

it is easier this way   not knowing   for knowing even one thing
no matter how infinitesimal   is a pandora's box full of meaning
and maybe this is the bitter pill   no one dares to swallow

The New York Quarterly Foundation, Inc.
New York, New York

Poetry Magazine

Since 1969

Edgy, fresh, groundbreaking, eclectic—voices from all walks of life.

Definitely NOT your mama's poetry magazine!

The *New York Quarterly* has been defining the term contemporary American poetry since it's first craft interview with W. H. Auden.

Interviews • Essays • and of course, lots of poems.

www.nyquarterly.org

No contest! That's correct, NYQ Books are NO CONTEST to other small presses because we do not support ourselves through contests. Our books are carefully selected by invitation only, so you know that NYQ Books are produced with the same editorial integrity as the magazine that has brought you the most eclectic contemporary American poetry since 1969.

Books

nyqbooks.org

poetry at the edge™

www.ingramcontent.com/pod-product-compliance
Lightning Source LLC
LaVergne TN
LVHW061346060426
835512LV00012B/2586